PERS PECT IVES

TAKING A DIFFERENT LOOK

BRITTNEY DAVIS

Ready Writer Books

To my Father in heaven, Thank you for sobriety of the mind. Thank you for clearing up the fog. Thank you for proper introduction and clarification to your word. Thank you for your unfailing love. Thank you for your mercy. Thank you for your Kindness. Thank you for YOUR Perspective.

Contents

III   Prayer & Faith

Preface

Throughout my life I was always able to see the other side of things. The unpopular opinions, the thoughts of others, and the possibility of what others couldn't necessarily see. I believe that it is crucial to be able to see another person's *perspective* and offer a challenge and light to what they are unable to see, as well as someone being able to challenge what we cannot see. Over the past year, I have been pulling back from a lot of what I thought I knew about Christianity. I started seeing a lot of content on social media that provoked me and instead of getting immediately offended I would ask God questions. Instead of immediately responding I would research. In fact, when I would go to post a status or video I would feel the pull to "put it in the book."

What I've learned over this past year is that our frame of reference, (which is the context and content of what we are built on); Our thoughts, our culture, and upbringing, all play apart in how we process what we take in. Not only our familial frame of reference, but our religious frame of reference can be damaging to how we see God. If we read scripture from our perspective, we can miss so much and experience an even greater consequence, which is not even really knowing our Savior.

I also learned the importance of unlearning what was an incorrect foundation. I had to be ok with questioning what wasn't scriptural and what wasn't intended for us a believers. I had to be ok with looking at scripture from God's perspective and from his intention.

Through this journey he allowed me to view him from the position of his child, and to see his heart. I pray the same happens for you as you read.

Lastly, I want to forewarn you: be cautious in how you engage with the contents of this book. If you view God in a certain way you may read it in a condemning tone and that is not the intention. If you view God in another way you may you may read it and think "God isn't that merciful or God isn't that 'soft." I want to suggest having an objective view.

For a moment, set aside your doctrine, denomination, and predisposed beliefs to examine what might be a different shift in your perspective.

I

Foundations and Frameworks

1

Is There Grace Available?

Luke 23:39-43
[39] One of the criminals who were hanged railed at him, saying, "Are you not the Christ? Save yourself and us!" [40] But the other rebuked him, saying, "Do you not fear God, since you are under the same sentence of condemnation? [41] And we indeed justly, for we are receiving the due reward of our deeds; but this man has done nothing wrong." [42] And he said, "Jesus, remember me when you come into your kingdom." [43] And he said to him, "Truly, I say to you, today you will be with me in paradise."

Am I alone in thinking that this time in life has been pretty heavy? It's been difficult to navigate. What makes it difficult is the disjointed belief system in the body of Christ. As a body we should be members that are moving together in unity. So, what happens when the body is trying to move in different ways at the same time? We run the risk of presenting the image of a body trying to walk and move with broken bones. A structure

3

of a skeleton that is damaged. (1 Corinthians 12:20-27)

An ideology that has caused me to take a pause and study is: "God loves us no matter what." That has been hard for me to digest. I was following some prophets who were heavy on the rebuke, and others who were heavy on grace which prompted me to study Jesus' walk.

I used to marvel at the prophetic and stock up on prophetic words, just wanting to know if I was in right standing with God. It was a breath of fresh air to discover that there was grace available to me, but it was and is still hard to reconcile that. I still find it difficult when I hear grace messages. "Am I being too easy on myself? Is there grace available to me? Does God really care about what I'm concerned with what I am concerned with. Am I weak because I'm fearful of what others are constantly warning about? Would I be able to last walking with Jesus while he was here on earth?"

I heard a song that prompted this writing. The lyrics were: "God, don't give up on me yet, I know I'm not your best bet but I'm trying." The questions in my mind started again: "is this song even biblical? Is it too grace heavy?" Is "grace heavy" even a thing? I just want to be as strong as the people who have received difficult warnings with joy and excitement. I want to not be so easily shaken. I want to believe that God loves me. I want to believe that he's ok with my faith and that it's ok to grow into it.

When thinking more about the song after sitting with it for a while, I immediately thought of Peter. How when Jesus told

4

the disciples that one of them would betray him, Peter said "surely it's not me." Jesus immediately said "I tell you the truth before the rooster crows, you'll deny me three times. When Jesus appeared to Peter after the resurrection, he asked Peter 3 times "do you love me?" Peter responded three times "you know I do". Jesus told him to feed his sheep and I immediately seen an example of restoration in that encounter.

A lot of us, because of our carnal understanding of what parenting *should* look like, and also because we were beat into salvation due to condemnation can't fathom God extending grace to those who have done the unthinkable. We forget about the one on the cross next to Jesus who believed and was promised eternal life close to the last moment of his life. There were no more works for him to do, and he was guilty.

My point is that there *has* to be an acceptance of grace. No matter how you came to Christ. The revelation of grace is crucial.

Reflection:
In what areas do I not believe that God's grace applies to me?

Prayer:
Father, sometimes it's difficult to navigate this world with all of the doctrines and opinions. Today I pray that. you would open up my mind to receive your word, correct interpretation, and clarity. I pray that you reveal to me the true revelation concerning the grace that is

available to me without the extra noise. Help me to be open to receiving your love through grace and not automatically condemn myself.

FURTHER REFLECTION

2

Watch What You Eat

Matthew 16:6-12

⁶ Jesus said to them, "Watch and beware of the leaven of the Pharisees and Sadducees." ⁷ And they began discussing it among themselves, saying, "We brought no bread." ⁸ But Jesus, aware of this, said, "O you of little faith, why are you discussing among yourselves the fact that you have no bread? ⁹ Do you not yet perceive? Do you not remember the five loaves for the five thousand, and how many baskets you gathered? ¹⁰ Or the seven loaves for the four thousand, and how many baskets you gathered? ¹¹ How is it that you fail to understand that I did not speak about bread? Beware of the leaven of the Pharisees and Sadducees." ¹² Then they understood that he did not tell them to beware of the leaven of bread, but of the teaching of the Pharisees and Sadducees.

Jesus told the disciples "don't eat what the Pharisees serve." We live in a culture of consumption. Just because it's placed in front of us doesn't mean that we have to eat it. If we are not careful, what we're consuming can consume us. Every diet isn't meant for everybody.

Without vetting what we believe is healthy teaching we can ingest poison that is outdated, lacks nourishment, and has no nutritional value. The difference between organic and conventional foods is that conventional foods are sprayed with things to kill what's naturally occurring in the environment around it. Organic produce is in its purest form. The same is true for the word of God. If tampered with, (taken out of text, not studied properly, used in evil ways) the original natural intention can be lost. The result of that is that we don't get to know the real character of God. The traditions of men vs. the Doctrine of God is a comparison of what we need to choose in our walk with God.

The traditions of men while it could have good intentions could also be a hindrance to the Doctrine of God. The Pharisees thought that they were right in upholding the law, which isn't a bad thing, but they couldn't recognize Jesus, who was God was among them. Colossians 2:1-4 says that the full assurance of understanding and the knowledge of God's mystery *is* Christ. It says that all of the treasures of wisdom and knowledge are hidden in him. Because of their pride in thinking that they knew the law so well, they missed that everything else they needed was right with them.

How can we be sure that we are digesting what was intended?

1. Get background information on scripture.

2. Look up the meaning of words in scripture.
3. Pray for understanding.
4. Be willing to be WRONG.
5. Be willing to cast aside previous interpretations and things learned from others.
6. Stop reading scripture in your current cultural context.

Context clears up confusion. Proper context/timelines help to clear up any confusion in scripture. Contexts bring clarity, seek the context to get clear understanding.

Reflection:
What traditions am I holding on to that are a hindrance to God's plan?

Prayer:
Father, I pray today for a detox of anything that I've eaten that's not from you. I ask that you instruct me on how to study, what is from you, and what is incorrect from man. I come to you asking that you remove any confusion, anything that has discouraged me from following you, and anything that has contributed to an incorrect foundation.

FURTHER REFLECTION

3

A Chaotic Home

Acts 15:36-41

[36] And after some days Paul said to Barnabas, "Let us return and visit the brothers in every city where we proclaimed the word of the Lord, and see how they are." [37] Now Barnabas wanted to take with them John called Mark. [38] But Paul thought best not to take with them one who had withdrawn from them in Pamphylia and had not gone with them to the work. [39] And there arose a sharp disagreement, so that they separated from each other. Barnabas took Mark with him and sailed away to Cyprus, [40] but Paul chose Silas and departed, having been commended by the brothers to the grace of the Lord. [41] And he went through Syria and Cilicia, strengthening the churches.

I grew up in a large family, my grandmother had 11 children. Sometimes holidays could get a bit chaotic with all of the loud talking and disagreements. To an outsider it could be intimidating. They might be worried about if someone is hurting someone's feelings or if a familial tie is beyond repair. To a family friend who is not familiar with the dynamics of the relationship, and is holding the family to a high expectation, it could cause them to look at the family differently or not want to engage further.

Sometimes it seems that we as the body of Christ are sitting in the house arguing. Debating. Pointing fingers. Pushing, fighting. Etc.… and the father has already commissioned us to go. Similarly in another example, we may bring people into these houses and communities that are full of discord and debates that aren't fruitful and expect them to sit and make themselves at home. So, what's happening to the harvest as we do this?

Jesus says in Matthew 9:37 "the harvest is plentiful, but the laborers are few." I looked up what happens if you don't harvest in time? "A late harvest can also cause plants to terminate or stop producing as they complete their reproduction process. Fully mature vegetables that are left on a plant also attract more disease and insect problems." In the opening scripture Paul and Barnabas disagreed and *separated* and Paul went on and strengthened the church. They didn't stay stuck running in circles in their arguments with one another. They didn't continue on arguing about who was right in what doctrine they believed. They separated and went on to work for God.

I believe that we should take a look within ourselves and end the fruitless arguments on social media *and* the fruitless arguments in our hearts (because that's a thing lol). I often have internal arguments with others and although I don't debate online, the temptation is there. In the end most of the time I consider others who may become confused or how it may present a stumbling block. I try to consider whether a response will be beneficial or just an addition to the ego that confirms what I know.

Maybe we need to take a note and separate from our doctrine arguments and continue bringing people into the family. A healthy one.

Reflection:
What fight am I committed to that in the grand scheme of things, doesn't really matter?

Prayer:
Father, if I have had the wrong heart concerning disagreements with my brothers and sisters in Christ, I ask for forgiveness. If there has been anyone in the harvest that has been neglected because I wanted to be right instead of just being an extension of you, I ask that you have mercy on me. I pray that you would shift my focus from arguing to just sharing you. I pray that you would give me the heart to speak of you when prompted and give me the mind to be concerned with what you're concerned with.

FURTHER REFLECTION

4

Hey, Focus.

Luke 9: 46-48

[46] An argument arose among them as to which of them was the greatest. [47] But Jesus, knowing the reasoning of their hearts, took a child and put him by his side [48] and said to them, "Whoever receives this child in my name receives me, and whoever receives me receives him who sent me. For he who is least among you all is the one who is great."

Luke 22:24-30

[24] A dispute also arose among them, as to which of them was to be regarded as the greatest. [25] And he said to them, "The kings of the Gentiles exercise lordship over them, and those in authority over them are called benefactors. [26] But not so with you. Rather, let the greatest among you become as the youngest, and the leader as one who serves. [27] For who is the greater, one who reclines at table or one who serves? Is it not the one who reclines at table? But I am among you as the one who serves.[28] "You are those

who have stayed with me in my trials, [29] and I assign to you, as my Father assigned to me, a kingdom, [30] that you may eat and drink at my table in my kingdom and sit on thrones judging the twelve tribes of Israel.

Looking at these scriptures the disciples were in a dispute asking who among them was the greatest. The Bible uses the word "dispute" which is "quarrelsome" in the original language. The temptation when among someone great can be comparison. The temptation is to compare yourself to what you see in hopes that you can reach their level or achieve what they have. The temptation is coveting gifts or status.

I believe that in he context of what's happening, *focus* is the main issue here. In both instances the disciples are in the middle of seeing Jesus perform a miracle, and the Lord's Supper. The conversation diverts to who is going to be the best among them. Just like the disciples we've been concerned about the wrong things a lot of the time. Specifically in the climate that we are in now, if someone wants to be the greatest, they could build that themselves.

Titles and gifts have been used to prop people up on unsteady pedestals. People have been wrapped up in warped identities and confusion. How can I confidently write these things? I remember being in a church culture where there was a great temptation to take in the praises of men as validation of my standing with Christ. I was once tempted and sometimes still am tempted to take what I've produced on a stage and compare myself to the "greatest." I was tempted to use my title to validate my rank among those who I looked up to and wanted to mirror. That's not the rubric that was intended for us. The rubric is always our hearts lined up to the Word, and if our hearts are not solely focused on loving God with all of us then what we produce doesn't matter.

As I write, I believe that I hear Holy Spirit speaking:

"I never meant for this unholy hierarchy to take precedent over my will." If you aren't careful and if you don't repent the quicksand foundation that you have built upon will leave you in ruin. You must focus. You have turned my house into a circus, endorsed & constructed secret societies that are impenetrable to those who actually want me. Performing tricks disguised as miracles. Disguising fortune telling as prophecy. All in the name of validating a title that will eventually pass away. You've put yourself before others in the name of honor. You've backbitten, gas-lit, and shunned the future generations to get all of your shine. Have you not already received your reward on earth? Repent and ask me to search your heart. Repent and ask me to cleanse your heart. It is time that my will is priority. To the pure in heart do not be tempted by the facades and displays of power you see. For truly this is a form of godliness, but they deny the power."

We shouldn't aim to be the greatest in any capacity. Our hearts should be that we want God to be the greatest.

Reflection:
Where have I been tempted to compare myself to others in order to validate gifting and/or status that will one day pass away?

Prayer:
Father, I dismiss every thought that would tempt me to pit myself against others. Any thought to compare myself, exalt myself, or make a goal to be "great," I ask that you remove them. Help me to remain low, humble, and meek. Most of all help me to be secure in my identity as your son or daughter. Help me to remain in reflection of the greatest in your kingdom and mirror their example.

FURTHER REFLECTION

5

The Skillful Builder

1 Samuel 16:7
But the Lord said to Samuel, "Do not look on his appearance or on the height of his stature, because I have rejected him. For the Lord sees not as man sees: man looks on the outward appearance, but the Lord looks on the heart."

1 Corinthians 3:10-11
[10] According to the grace of God given to me, like a skilled[a] master builder I laid a foundation, and someone else is building upon it. Let each one take care how he builds upon it. [11] For no one can lay a foundation other than that which is laid, which is Jesus Christ.

I have a habit of searching for homes on Zillow. Very recently I came across a few properties that were listed as new constructions. Some of the new construction homes were brand new inside out. Some of them were recently renovated, but two of them caught my eye especially. There was one home that was beautiful on the outside. Modern design, Pine Door, Black and gray siding. I just *knew* that the inside was about to be immaculate.

I kept thinking "wow this price is really low for a new construction with such a breath-taking exterior. The whole time I was in anticipation of scrolling to see more photos, but there were no more photos and as I read the description, I seen that it said, "exterior is complete, and the interior is in the rough stage."

Initially I experienced disappointment but was not surprised as the price matched what the explanation offered. Also, the initial revelation that came to mind was "something beautiful on the outside but a mess on the inside isn't worth much." I was quickly corrected as I thought about what Holy Spirit wanted to share. I heard the Lord *actually* saying, "The value once completed will double or triple."

The description also said, *"Built with unique design and ready for your completion."*

1. Why do we so quickly go to the negative about everything. Have we conditioned our hearts to think the worse? Have we been overloaded with teachings that only tell us how awful we are? I honestly don't remember that being the sole theme of Jesus' teaching for those that had the right heart.
2. We were all built with unique design, with God's intention of completing His work.

Unfortunately, we treat people like this. We see a flaw or hear of an advertised flaw from others and want to immediately write them off (I'm talking to me too). We forget that we *all* are a work in progress, and at some point, someone might have wanted to write us off too by not seeing the investment and pay off that we would be eventually. The property's structure, frame, and foundation were intact which means that the inside could possibly just need a few minor cosmetic changes or even a big renovation. Either way, the builder can handle it.

So, when we see things that we initially think are valuable but don't present as such let's remember these things that the word shares with us:

For I am **confident of this very thing, that He who began a good work among you will complete it by the day of Christ Jesus. Philippians 1:6**

Before I formed you in the womb I knew you, and before you were born, I consecrated you; I appointed you a prophet to the nations." Jeremiah 1:5

Reflection:
Are there any areas in my life or the lives of others that I don't believe that God can renovate? If So, why do I believe that?

Prayer:
Father, help me not to look at the negative and shift my perspective from pessimistic to hopeful. I pray that you open up my eyes to the work that you are completing in myself and those around me. I ask that you help me to

handle what you've built carefully, leaning into what *you* have said instead of my initial thoughts. Help me to remember that you're always looking on the inside, not the outside, and when I am over critical of even myself, help me to remember that you are perfect in all of your ways, even what you create.

FURTHER REFLECTION

6

Be Careful with Your Weapon

Hebrews 4:12
For the word of God is living and active, sharper than any two-edged sword, piercing to the division of soul and of spirit, of joints and of marrow, and discerning the thoughts and intentions of the heart.

The Bible describes the word of God as a sword. Ephesians 6:17 talks about the whole armor of God and the sword of the spirit which is the word of God.

If you're like me, when I heard the word sword I thought of a long sword that slices. However the word sword in Hebrews is machairan which is actually a short short sword or dagger. This is why it's associated with piercing instead of slicing.

A sharp sword/knife cuts smoothly. So even though there is pain from the cut, the healing might be nicer. A sharp blade is easier to control and causes less injuries. A dull sword/knife would leave someone rugged and bloody. It doesn't cut smoothly, and causes injury. Sharpening our swords can look like: proper study, humility when reading, and listening to Holy Spirit for the correct application.

There was a time in college where I was reading the scripture about how God's sheep know his voice and another they won't follow. Well, somehow I got that scripture mixed up with John 8:43-44 where Jesus is speaking to the Pharisees who did not believe him. He said "Why don't you understand what I say, you are of your father the devil." The mistake that I made is I stopped before the completion of the scripture, I didn't have the proper context of the scripture, and I became distraught because I thought that the scripture was saying that if I didn't hear the audible voice of God then I wasn't his child. Thank God for someone that was more mature than me in the faith being able to teach me the correct way to look at those passages.

It's imperative that we use the word in the correct way to not leave ourselves or other people bloody. We must make sure we are using the word in context. We must make sure we continue to be sharp with the word, so as to cut smoothly. We must study and be open to learning from Holy Spirit so that our perspective is that of God and not tradition.

Reflection:
Have I left anyone bloody by improperly using the word?
What have I learned from that?

Prayer:
Father, I pray that you would help me to use wisdom

while using my weapon of the word. I ask that you would make me skillful in using your word to learn you, teach you, and love you. I pray that your word would properly heal, correct, and readjust my thinking. Please help me to sharpen my sword with Holy Spirit guiding me as I read.

FURTHER REFLECTION

7

The Proper Build

1 Peter 2: 4-6
4 As you come to him, a living stone rejected by men but in the sight of God chosen and precious, 5 you yourselves like living stones are being built up as a spiritual house, to be a holy priesthood, to offer spiritual sacrifices acceptable to God through Jesus Christ. 6 For it stands in Scripture: "Behold, I am laying in Zion a stone, a cornerstone chosen and precious,and whoever believes in him will not be put to shame."

A strong foundation is crucial to the framework of us as a temple of God and our belief system. If your foundation has cracks or isn't solid, then the structure can fall. So, if our beliefs aren't built upon the sole foundation of Jesus Christ then we will likely get into situations where our faith is in trouble or it's harder to stay rooted in him.

If we have a foundation and then we try to build without the corner the structure will fall, but if we build around the cornerstone the structure will be solid. Verse 5 says that we are living stones being built up to be a spiritual house. That means that we are all being laid together to be built on Jesus as the body of Christ.

We aren't alone in this walk and we should be working together to be willing to be used to build God's house. What does that look like? Sometimes we have the wrong priorities and the wrong focus. We focus on tradition, bylaws, etc. and even though we may come out of those things to focus on Jesus, sometimes there's a residue which is why it's important to allow God to press those things out of us.

In 1 Corinthians 3 Paul is talking to a church who is bragging about who they follow between Paul and Apollos. Paul tells them that he and Apollos are only men, servants of Jesus. He starts talking about how what he has taught and what he has built is only built on the foundation of Jesus.

1 Corinthians 3:10
By the grace God has given me, I laid a foundation as a wise builder, and someone else is building on it. But each one should build with care. 11 For no one can lay any foundation other than the one already laid, which is Jesus Christ. 12 If anyone builds on this foundation using gold, silver, costly stones, wood, hay or straw, 13 their work will be shown for what it is, because the Day will bring it to light. It will be revealed with fire, and the fire will test the quality of each person's work. 14 If what has been built survives, the builder will receive a reward.

We have to be careful about what we are building. We have to be careful about what we are using to build it. We have to make the important things become important again. How do we do that? We have to get to know Jesus. Not who people tell us who he is, but we have to study his heart, his actions, who he talked to, why he talked to them in the way that he did, and what he stood for.

How do we get to know Jesus? The word, but we have to be careful not to read to understand from our preexisting frame of reference. A frame of reference is how we view the world based on what we have experienced.

We have to be careful not to handle God's people and honestly ourselves through *our* frame of reference. Our frame of reference can pollute our perception and interpretation of the word, and of others around us.

How many times have you been in conversations with fellow believers and they're describing something about the Lord and in your heart, you're saying, "that's not the God that I know!" It's because if we have had a negative experience with a father and we hear the word father we might apply our definition of father to God.

Studying scripture from the framework of your culture, or your humanity, or the way your mind works is a breeding ground for false teaching. When you make your intellect, culture, and your way of thinking your guide, you will potentially filter everything thing through that way of thought which can be poisonous for you and others to digest.

Reflection:
Does my foundation and framework need to be
reassessed and/or rebuilt? How do I know this?

Prayer:
Father, I pray that if I've built anything without you being
the foundation that you forgive me. I ask that you help
me to identify false teaching that I've submitted to. I ask
that you help me to identify anything about you that I've
misinterpreted. I pray that you would help me to restore
the proper foundation to every area of my life. I pray that
if any area of my life is built on the wrong intentions,
heart, or priority that you would forgive me and redirect
my path to the proper place. I pray that you rebuild any
vision or idea that you've given me from the ground up. I
submit my life to you and ask that you correct the course
of my mind and heart.

FURTHER REFLECTION

8

Look Again

Hebrews 4:12
12 For the word of God is alive and active. Sharper than any double-edged sword, it penetrates even to dividing soul and spirit, joints and marrow; it judges the thoughts and attitudes of the heart.

A common temptation when hearing a popular scripture is thinking "I've heard this before" without fully engaging with an open ear that could lead to further revelation. We all know the scriptures that we've committed to memory for encouragement, but a lot of times those scriptures have so much more to them. I've had to examine my heart several times as I'm on the journey of reading the bible through listening. It's easy to check out when you're familiar with a story or verse but the truth is, if the word of God is active and we serve a living all knowing God, there's no way at first or even tenth glance that we will be able to fully grasp *all* of what the word of God is saying. I have read what seems to be the most "simple" scriptures and because they were out of context or I didn't understand the historical background, when I read it again it had a different meaning.

Humility is definitely a necessity when taking the word into consideration. It's important to read seeking to understand what God wants us to know, and seeking to have a greater understanding than reading from a perspective of thinking that we know it all.

When we realize that there can be nothing surface level about the words of the creator of heaven and earth, we invite Him into our studies allowing Him to share His heart instead of leaving the scriptures up to assumption.

A part of knowing the heart of God when it comes to scripture is knowing the cultural and historical context of the time period. Reading from your own cultural context will ensure that we miss so much.

So, take another look...I'm sure we will all be comforted by what we see.

Reflection:
What's a scripture that I became too familiar with without studying? What are sayings and phrases that I live by that might not be biblical?

Prayer:
Father I pray that if I've become too common or familiar with you that you would forgive me. I ask that as I open your word, that I would be able to see new things that you want to reveal to me. I pray that you would show me what

I need from you that's beyond the surface level. I pray that I would be able to see what was familiar in the past, as you originally intended and that you would correct anything that I've learned that isn't from you.

FURTHER REFLECTION

9

False gods.

Colossians 2:8
8 See to it that no one takes you captive by philosophy and empty deceit, according to human tradition, according to the elemental spirits[a] of the world, and not according to Christ.

Jeremiah 15:16
When your words came, I ate them;
they were my joy and my heart's delight,
for I bear your name,
Lord God Almighty.

What do you think of when you hear the term "false god?" As Christians we often identify "false gods" as gods outside of Yaweh or the One true and living God. We often think of other religious gods as false before we consider that a misrepresentation of our God is a false god. If not completely a false god, then a misrepresentation can definitely represent a false ideology. I like to compare it to someone getting wrong information about you and being coincorrect about your character. If we are learning from false teachers and what they speak about God is false, then what we worship is then false. Not in a sense of us believing that God isn't real, but in a sense of not having the correct information about him to apply it to our lives.

We hear things, take it for law and reproduce false teaching as a result. Next thing you know we are 20 years into our walk with God and a spark goes off that says "that's not even what that means and that's not even who God is"

When we hear teaching we should always take time to look deeper and listen for what Holy Spirit is trying to reveal through the scripture. We should be bold enough to believe differently if needed. Sometimes we make the error of being sold bad theology for someone who is popular or well trusted, and they may have good intentions. The goal is to know the *true* identity of God, the *true* heart of God, the *true* intention of God, and the *true* love of God.

Studying is so important, as well as filtering what we consume through the proper interpretation of scripture. We have to be bold enough to help others through wrong thinking patterns.

I thank God for the chaplain in college who helped me to understand scripture after I came to her thinking that I wasn't God's daughter because I thought that I couldn't hear his voice. We have to be bold enough to walk people through the scriptures and help them learn tools in studying the bible so that they don't get swept up in the enemies plan of confusion.

I thank God for friends who I can have those tough "what do you think this scripture is saying?" conversations. Community is important in shaping your perspective of scripture. The wrong community will have you down a path of pride by implementing structure around false teaching. It is important that we devote ourselves to studying in addition to the teaching that we receive.

What I mean is that if we studied, instead of taking in the word at the surface we would have a better chance of knowing our real God.

Reflection:
Is there any area that I can identify now, where I believe I've exposed myself to lies about God? Are there things that I have believed about God that can be challenged with the Word?

Prayer:
Father, I pray that you would help me to know you in the truest way. I ask that as I read your word, you expose any lies that have been planted in my heart about you. I ask that you would help me to understand your character, your love, your standards, and your word. I pray that you would shine a light on who you are as I continue to study you.

FURTHER REFLECTION

II

Perspectives and Outlooks

10

Is There Error in Your Perspective of Christ?

Matthew 22:15-45

Over the past two months I've been listening to the audio bible. Immediately when listening to the beginning of the gospels, I noticed a common theme: the religious leaders were unwilling to set somethings aside in order to recognize Jesus for who he was. Given the historical context of who they were, they should have been in the position of receiving Jesus. They should have been expecting him.

So, I asked a question: "Why didn't the Sadducees and Pharisees believe that Jesus was the Messiah?

Throughout the gospels the Pharisees question Jesus about what he and the disciples are doing on the sabbath, they question his knowledge of the law, they greet him with sarcasm. They were looking for the Messiah to look different. They weren't willing to set aside their belief system to engage with the Messiah who was right in front of them. However, the people who were actively looking for Jesus found him. The people looking for salvation found it. The people who were looking for debate, argument, and the opportunity to be critical and found that.

When encountering Jesus their heart position wasn't "I'm looking for the Savior" They were instead engulfed in their position that they thought gave them great accolades and recognition. They were concerned with testing, and committed to misunderstanding Jesus instead of leaning into everyone that was testifying of his greatness. This hindered their ability to humble themselves and recognize that they still should've been seeking their savior. In the midst of keeping the law, they forgot that Jesus was coming.

As we open up these conversations about our perspective of the gospel and our walk with Christ. I want to challenge you to first identify the areas where you graze over or ignore Jesus as Lord and minimize him to be distant. How do we minimize Jesus to be distant and not Lord of our lives? By not acknowledging that he is present. **(A present help in the time of trouble, Psalm 46:1).** By not acknowledging that he's in the walk of life with us. Sometimes we've treated Jesus like he's a fictional character in scripture.

Sometimes we minimized him as Lord, and just set him aside as if the interactions that we read about in scripture are not applicable.

Jesus is the Word. (John 1). The word is Active. Hebrews 4:12

As we study to change any error in our perspective of God. Let's first shift his position in our lives. Let's meditate and focus on placing him in his rightful spot in our lives. Let's look for him.

Reflection:

What is my heart's position and expectation when I encounter Jesus in the Word, in life, and in prayer? Do I see Jesus as Lord, or do I minimize him in my everyday life?

Prayer:

Father, as I am becoming open to challenging my own perspective of your word, I ask that you would shine a light to what you want me to know about you. I ask that you would help me to remove any error in my thinking about you and your word. I pray that my position before you would be that of humility. Thank you for your grace and help in seeing you the way that you want to be seen.

FURTHER REFLECTION

11

An Appetite Without the Capacity

Matthew 6:25-34

[25] "Therefore I tell you, do not be anxious about your life, what you will eat or what you will drink, nor about your body, what you will put on. Is not life more than food, and the body more than clothing? [26] Look at the birds of the air: they neither sow nor reap nor gather into barns, and yet your heavenly Father feeds them. Are you not of more value than they? [27] And which of you by being anxious can add a single hour to his span of life?[a] [28] And why are you anxious about clothing? Consider the lilies of the field, how they grow: they neither toil nor spin, [29] yet I tell you, even Solomon in all his glory was not arrayed like one of these. [30] But if God so clothes the grass of the field, which today is alive and tomorrow is thrown into the oven, will he not much more clothe you, O you of little faith? [31] Therefore do not be anxious, saying, 'What shall we eat?' or 'What shall we drink?' or 'What shall we wear?' [32] For the Gentiles seek after all these things, and your heavenly Father knows that you need them all.

³³ But seek first the kingdom of God and his righteousness, and all these things will be added to you. ³⁴ "Therefore do not be anxious about tomorrow, for tomorrow will be anxious for itself. Sufficient for the day is its own trouble.

This is a popular scripture when we as believers are overwhelmed, stressed, and worried. I know in the past I've said: "Read Matthew 6:25-34!" when anyone came to me expressing those feelings. It's great to have access to these encouraging words during those times, but instead of just settling for being worried, anxious or overwhelmed we have to look at why we may be feeling this way. Being overwhelmed or wanting information that we don't have, can come from wanting control. Wanting control is a result of fear. Fear is an enemy of faith. Wanting to control every aspect of your life is wanting to be Lord. Do we really trust God to take the reins, or do we think we can do it better? An interesting temptation that I've been able to see within myself and in others is that with access to information, we believe that we should have knowledge about *everything*.

Our capacity for what is given to us through the media and other outlets has been overloaded with the 24-hour access, rabbit holes, algorithms etc. Not only media but the access that we have to voices that were never supposed to be in our ears is problematic as well.

The word clearly tells us not to worry about tomorrow. The word points to God's heart towards us telling us that if God intricately cares about the lilies of the field and the birds of the air,"how much more does he care about us, as his children and his creation?"

I believe that it is wise to be careful of what we ingest and take in at this time. What you try to control but don't have the power to, can push you into fear and anxiety.

We have to believe that our father will provide for us, whether that be food, peace, joy, etc. If you can't settle or digest what you consume once it's ingested, then it could be unhealthy.

There are prophetic warnings and directions from God that we should be obedient to, in fact the word says ""For the Lord GOD does nothing without revealing his secret to his servants the prophets." Amos 3:7 but in hearing warnings from the prophets that does not mean that we should fear. When we try to handle what we can't control it will often consume us. Most of all, we have to know that we don't have the capacity to take in all of what God is knowledgeable of.

He's all knowing, and because of that we don't have to be. Do not worry about tomorrow.

Reflection:
What have I been stuffing myself with that I don't have room for? What information do I want that's a reflection of my lack of trust in God?

Prayer:
Father, I give you every worry and fear that may have

consumed my mind no matter how small. I give all control over to you and pray that you would help my unbelief when it comes to trusting you in difficult times. I pray that you give me wisdom on what to take into my heart and mind. I ask that your perfect love would cast out all fear.

FURTHER REFLECTION

12

Which Character Do You Play?

Romans 12:3
³ For by the grace given to me I say to everyone among you not to think of himself more highly than he ought to think, but to think with sober judgment, each according to the measure of faith that God has assigned.

There's a song that says:

"So often we look at the story of David and see ourselves as David, when really we are the sheep that were unaware that a bear was even there."

When we look at the gospel and then look at ourselves it is important to humbly acknowledge which part we are playing in the narrative. We want to see ourselves as Jesus-like automatically, but could we the unbeliever? Are we the sinner?Are we the disciple? Are we the desperate, with faith seeking Christ's interventions? Are we the Pharisee unable to see the miraculous work of God through Jesus because of foggy colored contacts? It's only after embracing this honesty that growth can occur.

If we take an honest look at the body of Christ, at the moment an "exposure" happens we are bringing them before whomever to yell crucify them. How quickly we forget the woman caught in adultery. How quickly we forget restoring our brother or sister in a spirit of gentleness. How quickly we forget Peter's restoration, and the grace given to doubting Thomas.

Acknowledging what role we are playing helps to correctly assess where we are in our walk with God. We will not be perfect, but seeing ourselves higher than we are can create a false sense of entitlement and gives us a mind to think that we can judge others who are falling short. The truth is, even those who are struggling in sin as a believer can receive the grace of God. To look down on them in a sense of pride like we are perfect is an injustice to them, when we weren't even worthy when we came to Christ. We still are *only* worthy through the blood of Jesus Christ. Peter, having heard "if you deny me before men I'll deny you before my father" still denied Jesus after confidently thinking that he would never do anything like that.

We have to be intentional in being humble before the Lord, realizing that we are nothing without him, that we are sheep that need to be led, that we are one decision away from those that we judge the worst. We have to know that it is only the blood of Jesus that was shed that allows us to stand in high places. We have to know that it was not our own wisdom that has helped us to flee from trouble or accomplish what we have, but it was God's grace. It's only by grace that we are saved. So that we boast in Christ and not who we think that we are.

Reflection:
Which character am I currently playing ?

Prayer:
Father, if I have been playing any role that is not true to my character I pray that you reveal it so that I can be aware of where I stand with you. I pray that humility would wash over my heart and that you remind me that it is because of your unfailing love that I can stand before you. I pray that you help to remind me that it is by your grace that I can interact and commune with you. Help me see my brothers and sisters and your children the way that you intend them to be, helping them to follow you by faith and not works.

FURTHER REFLECTION

13

A Cruel Lord?

Isaiah 63:7
I will recount the steadfast love of the Lord,
the praises of the Lord,
according to all that the Lord has granted us,
and the great goodness to the house of Israel
that he has granted them according to his compassion,
according to the abundance of his steadfast love.

I have heard people say, "Jesus wasn't nice," and in my immaturity I have interpreted that to mean that he's not approachable. I question in what context they've read the gospel. What has been interpreted as Jesus being "mean" has endorsed a church culture that isn't a mirror to how Jesus walked at all. Was he assertive? Absolutely. Stern? Yes. Direct? Yes. but Mean? Not at all.

I have even seen and have struggled myself with viewing the God of the old testament as cruel. The truth is that the old testament is full of *mercy*. The Israelite's since leaving Egypt struggled so badly with idolatry, with trusting that God wasn't there for them. They desired what was old because it was comfortable, and it did not require faith.

The bible records that the Lord's anger was kindled against them, and he wanted to destroy them more than several times. A lot of people stop there and that does not provide the full picture of who God is.

There was always an intercessor who prayed and reminded God of his promises to Israel. The Lord also always offered an opportunity for them to repent and move forward. Even after they entered the promised land and they continued to worship other gods, when they cried out the Lord responded. They would turn from their sin and turn back to it.

This isn't a justification for Israel, Paul says in Romans 7: Should we sin so that grace abounds? No. but we must remember that we often are *not* the intercessor, Moses, or Joshua in our lives.We are the people who *need* God to forgive us *again*.

It is sobering to think about how merciful God is towards us.

His mercy is absolutely a reflection of his KINDNESS. How much more are we supposed to show mercy to others. It should be easy, seeing as though we should be able to see how stained we were before encountering his kindness and love. Kindness breaks down to mean devotion, faithfulness, loyal, and merciful. Titus 3:4-7.

He has expressed his love for us. Jesus said that he didn't come to destroy the law, but he came to fulfill it because we can't keep it.

He stands in our place.

24 Now to him who is able to keep you from stumbling and to present you blameless before the presence of his glory with great joy, 25 to the only God, our Savior, through Jesus Christ our Lord, be glory, majesty, dominion, and authority, before all time[h] and now and forever. Amen.
Jude 1:24

Reflection:
Have I embraced the image and narrative of a God that isn't kind, full of mercy, and grace? Where did I get that idea from?

Prayer:
Father, help me to digest the fact that it is your joy to present me faultless through Jesus Christ. I ask that you help me to understand the true tone of your scripture when it comes to how you feel about me. I pray that you open my mind to receive all of the good that you have said, and that it's imparted into me to be confident in my relationship with you. I pray that your characteristics would jump out at me and that I would rest in your love for me. Thank you for your unfailing love and mercy.

FURTHER REFLECTION

14

Sometimes They'll Sort It Out Themselves

Acts 19
(Just read the whole thing)

The people of the community represented in this scripture were upset that the teachings of Paul caused their false god to lose credibility. Building idols was the livelihood of that area and how they made their money, but Paul had taught the gospel and many who worshipped the handmade god had turned to Jesus.

The people came together and it was chaotic, their idolatry and their will to keep their shrines and worship to their goddess caused them to be in chaos and it also caused them to be angry with Paul. Some people within the gathering did not even know why they were there, they just joined in with the crowd.

Paul wanted to go in the temple to defend himself, and the disciples urged him not to. The town clerk quieted the crowd and told them that they were in danger of being charged with rioting , because there was not a real cause for the commotion.

If Paul would've entered the theater, then there would have been cause to bring him before the court or he could've been condemned for condemning their god. But the timing of the disciples urging him not to go into the theater, allowed him to escape without war. The group of his enemies disassembled themselves due to their confusion causing chaos.

For perspective, God doesn't need you to defend him, sometimes a war that you created is the cause of your own delay.

Paul had another destination to go through to encourage the believers. There were people waiting for him, people that he had encouraged. Don't get caught up in quieting another person's chaos.

Reflection:
Is there a time where I remained untouched although I felt the pressure of an enemy in order to get me to where he wanted me? How can I remember that moving forward?

Prayer:
Father, help me to navigate the the battles that I may find myself in. I ask that you help me to remember to always ask for wisdom. I pray that you help me to realize that no one or nothing is more powerful than you. If there is any area of my life where I have engaged in warfare that has caused delay I pray that you reveal it and help me to

remember to seek you first in every decision.

FURTHER REFLECTION

15

The Beauty in an Audience of One

Matthew 14:22-33

[22] Immediately Jesus made the disciples get into the boat and go on ahead of him to the other side, while he dismissed the crowd. [23] After he had dismissed them, he went up on a mountainside by himself to pray. Later that night, he was there alone, [24] and the boat was already a considerable distance from land, buffeted by the waves because the wind was against it. [25] Shortly before dawn Jesus went out to them, walking on the lake. [26] When the disciples saw him walking on the lake, they were terrified. "It's a ghost," they said, and cried out in fear. [27] But Jesus immediately said to them: "Take courage! It is I. Don't be afraid." [28] "Lord, if it's you," Peter replied, "tell me to come to you on the water." [29] "Come," he said. Then Peter got down out of the boat, walked on the water and came toward Jesus. [30] But when he saw the wind, he was afraid and, beginning to sink, cried out, "Lord, save me!" [31] Immediately Jesus reached out his hand and caught him. "You of little faith," he said, "why did you doubt?"

³² And when they climbed into the boat, the wind died down. ³³ Then those who were in the boat worshiped him, saying, "Truly you are the Son of God."

Numbers don't always mean success. I think that some of us have highlighted large services, negating and diminishing small rooms, gatherings and intimate encounters. That's not to say that the glory of God cannot come into large spaces. Jesus himself was often in the company of large crowds teaching, healing, performing miracles, feeding etc.

I have been in rooms full of thousands of people, able to feel the tangible presence of God. (No, it wasn't the smoke machines lol). It was the surrendered heart of those yielded to the will of God. It was the obedience of *his* will being carried out. Not man's agenda, but what the heart of the father wanted to speak to *his* people.

So, I don't diminish large gatherings. In fact, I believe that as the Father looks on earth seeing thousands and thousands of people worshiping him, he is pleased. That's the whole point, right? To win the lost to a relationship with God through Jesus, to gather, and fellowship with one another.

I want to offer another perspective as well, that in those intimate teaching moments with the disciples attempting to walk on water, in the upper room when the thousands had dispersed, the mount of transfiguration, or after the Last Supper when Jesus' washed the disciples' feet, those moments were just as powerful.

Recently, I've struggled with searching for community, wondering when I'll find it and I've heard the heart of others doing the same. I've learned to find value in the moments that aren't often qualified as community.

So, if you aren't experiencing what you think you should in a room full of people, remember how God met you when no one else was there. How he used an individual who you had no relationship with to speak to you right on time. How he used a hug from an elder to comfort you. How he revealed to you a perfect scripture right on time.

If you're seeking community, consider the circle of three. The intimacy of you and the father, the company of one.

Reflection:
Have I had any moments where God met me with just him and I or with a small group? Did I consider that community? Why or why not?

Prayer:
Father help me to remember the intimate moments with you. I pray that you would call out to my heart in moments where I forget. I ask that you would help me to remember that you will always be there and you will never leave or forsake me. Father help me to remember that even when I don't have a tangible feeling you are always there. Thank you for placing others around me, but in moments where they may not be available, teach me how to silence the noise and hear your voice clearly.

FURTHER REFLECTION

16

Be Loving to the Blind

Galatians 6:1
Brothers,[a] if anyone is caught in any transgression, you who are spiritual should restore him in a spirit of gentleness. Keep watch on yourself, lest you too be tempted.

What you're about to read is not a criticism of God's beloved. We've talked about the legalists quite a bit so far. As I began to mature in the faith and read scripture in context, I started seeing the similarities between the legalists and certain denominations. I started to notice a doctrine that was not from the gospel, but from man. It was easy to become frustrated with the mistreatment of those who Jesus would've served by looking at scripture. It's easy to look at someone and judge them without impacting them, without asking their story, or engaging them in conversation.

I noticed that I was becoming more and more critical of the bride. More judgmental of the people that I wanted to have more grace. I had become a Pharisee to the Pharisees.

Then, someone asked me one day if I had grace for the prisoners and probationers that I worked with and I quickly said yes!!! No questions there. They deserve grace, we are too hard on them. We don't extend grace and mercy. We hold their charges over their heads as if they aren't serving or have served their time. We make it difficult for them to move on.

She said: "extend the same grace to the religious for they are imprisoned as well." That was a hard word to hear. I always thought "they should know better."

One of my favorite scriptures has become Galatians 6:1 " Brothers,[a] if anyone is caught in any transgression, you who are spiritual should restore him in a spirit of gentleness. Keep watch on yourself, lest you too be tempted."

The word Trespass is "paraptoma" in Greek which means fall away after being close-beside, i.e. a *lapse* (deviation) from the truth; an error, "slip up"; wrong doing that can be (relatively) *unconscious*, "non-deliberate."

So not only do we need to restore the sinner, but our brothers and sisters as well. Most modern day pharisees are BLIND. Jesus would speak openly in parables in their presence, and they would be unable to see what he was talking about. Matthew 23:26

It was Paul who needed Ananias after his encounter with Jesus. It was the Pharisees who after Pentecost cried "what have we done?" and needed the mercy and grace of the Apostles to restore them. Don't be like me. Show mercy to those who seemingly don't show mercy to others.

Reflection:
Do I have a hardened heart to those who need grace no matter where they are in their faith walk? What might be some areas where I can implement Galatians 6:1 better with my brothers and sisters in Christ ?

Prayers:
Father, I pray that you would help me to have compassion on those who don't see what you taught. I ask that you enable me to give grace to those I have deemed as unworthy. Help me to want you to restore those that don't agree with me. I pray that you help me to assist others without judgment and with love. Help me to realize that my fellow brothers and sisters need grace and restoration as well. I ask that you change my perspective when it comes to what angers me, even with a righteous anger teach me the right way to administrate it.

FURTHER REFLECTION

17

Do it Anyway

Matthew 21:23
²³ And when he entered the temple, the chief priests and the elders of the people came up to him as he was teaching, and said, "By what authority are you doing these things, and who gave you this authority?"

Matthew 15:1-3
Then Pharisees and scribes came to Jesus from Jerusalem and said, ² "Why do your disciples break the tradition of the elders? For they do not wash their hands when they eat." ³ He answered them, "And why do you break the commandment of God for the sake of your tradition?

I find it interesting that Jesus hears the question "who gave you the authority to…?" It mirrors a lot of what we see being taught today. It mirrors children being forsaken until they reach a certain age, although youth were prophets, kings, and pivotal parts of Jesus' Ministry. It mirrors people looking at their brothers and sisters and coming to the conclusion that they aren't ready to preach the gospel because they aren't packaged a certain way. It mirrors people unable to discern the value others bring despite not having the religious culture/language. It mirrors doctrine that says you have to be a certain way to be called. It mirrors people dancing, singing, and thinking in robotic mannerisms that give no glory to God. It mirrors social media spectators on videos asking: Why are you laying hands? Why are you doing miracles? Who sent you?

Some Christians have adopted the rules of the legalists that try to hinder the move of God. They question anything that doesn't look like what they're used to. There are people wondering why you may be doing something because they didn't endorse or lay hands or approve.

Legalists point fingers, while disciples extend hands. There was an instance when the disciples came to Jesus saying that someone was casting out demons in his name and they tried to stop them. Jesus corrected them and told them that anyone that wasn't against them was for them. (Mark 9:38-41)

One of the things that Jesus showed us through his interactions is that our obedience to God has to be more important than what others think. I've missed out on several opportunities because of the fear of man and because of false humility. We think that false humility keeps us safe from being prideful. People will affirm us, and give us opportunities and we reply "no, no, not me." "That was a great sermon," and we get into this playful banter where it feels good to compliment each other at the sake of diminishing what God has put inside of us. Humility is not thinking of ourselves as less than, but it's being low under

God. It's not exalting yourself above him. I pray boldness over this issue. I pray that we would be and do what God calls us to do no matter what doesn't make sense to others.

Much of what Jesus did on earth did not make sense to those around him. If Jesus had based the decisions that he made on those who questioned the validity of God's call on his life, would he have made it to the cross?

Am I diminishing the need for wise counsel, mentorship, or discipleship? No, but at some point, our will to be obedient to God's voice has to be greater than what man is saying.

Reflection:
What have I failed to obey due to voices that I've made louder than God's instructions?

Prayer:
Father, I repent if there is any area of my life that I have been disobedient to you due to me fearing man. I pray that through your mercy and grace you remind me of the ideas, plans, and instructions that you have given me to accomplish for your glory. I ask that you impart into me the wisdom and boldness to move forward when others don't understand. I pray that you remove all false humility and thrust me forward in the instructions that you have for me.

FURTHER REFLECTION

18

Save Myself?

Philippians 2:4
4 Let each of you look not only to his own interests, but also to the interests of others.

2 Corinthians 12:9-10
9 But he said to me, "My grace is sufficient for you, for my power is made perfect in weakness." Therefore I will boast all the more gladly of my weaknesses, so that the power of Christ may rest upon me. 10 For the sake of Christ, then, I am content with weaknesses, insults, hardships, persecutions, and calamities. For when I am weak, then I am strong.

Colossians 3:23-24
23 Whatever you do, work heartily, as for the Lord and not for men, 24 knowing that from the Lord you will receive the inheritance as your reward. You are serving the Lord Christ.

Self-Preservation. Is it biblical? Is it something that we should desire even though we are supposed to be reliant on God? Should we work so hard to preserve ourselves? I am not speaking of honoring our temples and taking care of them. But I am speaking of a culture that we have created where it's ok to seek protection of self, time, and not obey God because it may be inconvenient.

The truth is that we cannot protect ourselves from anything. God is our protector; he gives angels charge over us to keep us.(Psalm 91:11). So, the temptation to preserve ourselves, only causes us to lose out on more than we probably should.

For example, when I was pregnant with our first child, I would get so frustrated because people would constantly reach out to me asking me for prayer, not respecting boundaries that I tried to put in place. I would get irritated when people would just reach out me without asking how I was.It felt like a violation, because I thought it was my time to receive. I thought that I was entitled to being served and exempt from serving while in a challenging time.

The Lord started speaking to me about self-sacrifice and so I began to answer the phone, I began to pray when I didn't feel like it, and I began to just consider it a sacrifice to the Lord whenever I didn't have the strength to serve.

In reality there will always be a time and opportunity to serve when you are a believer, and sometimes it won't make sense or fit into our schedules.Sometimes it may be when we're going through tough situations. We may not be in the mood, or we will fell like we are there for others when no one is there for us.

We are in a time where boundaries are preached, and yes they are necessary, but the mistake that we make, especially in American culture is trying to hold tightly to some boundaries that we aren't supposed to have. We have been hurt by people and taken advantage of etc. and instead of healing completely so that we can extend ourselves when needed we close ourselves off and offer the minimal with caution. Without healing from those moments, we say no instead of discerning what could be something to say yes to. Our boundaries sometimes create a boundary to what God wants to do through us.

Sometimes a yes to something that we don't feel like doing can be beneficial for us. For me, sometimes it's as small as returning a phone call. I assume because I don't regularly get "how are you?" calls that the person wants something, when that's only a reflection of my past and not a correct perspective what's honestly going on.

Jesus absolutely went into times of seclusion but when it was time to offer himself, to heal, to pray, to teach, he did so. We have to rely on the father's strength to serve when we don't have the ability or the mind to.

Self-preservation only makes us hold on to what should be distributed. Instead, we can seek Holy Spirit on when and what to do.

Reflection:
Where have I been unwilling to trust God to be my

strength and increase my capacity?

Prayer:

Father, I pray that you would fix my heart to be obedient in the communities you've placed me in over my feelings. I ask that you give me the heart to bear the burdens of others, to love with sacrifice, and to lean into your example. I pray that I would grasp the knowledge that nothing that I do in my own strength is sustainable. I ask that you remove the negative stigma of "weakness," and help me to continue to lean into your strength so that I can be made strong when I "just don't feel like it." Father, help me to recognize that only you can preserve me.

FURTHER REFLECTION

III

Prayer & Faith

19

Do You Trust Me?

John 11:38
³⁸ Jesus therefore again groaning in himself cometh to the grave. It was a cave, and a stone lay upon it. ³⁹ Jesus said, Take ye away the stone. Martha, the sister of him that was dead, saith unto him, Lord, by this time he stinketh: for he hath been dead four days.
⁴⁰ Jesus saith unto her, Said I not unto thee, that, if thou wouldest believe, thou shouldest see the glory of God?

The opening scripture is from a familiar passage when Jesus raises Lazarus from the dead. The word "believe" occurs in this passage four times in the same context and it means to be persuaded, faith, trust, confidence, and fidelity. In this passage Jesus is asking over and over again "do you trust me?" "Do you trust that you're walking in the light when you're with me?" "Do you trust that when I am in a situation everything can change?"

As believer's sometimes we have a surface level understanding of the deity of Jesus and the power of Jesus but in hardships that we experience it's very easy to become drunken with the rhetoric of what's going on in our everyday lives.

Our belief in the power of God shows that we have history with him. Sometimes I've found that when so much negative is present, it's hard to sober up.

1 Peter 5:8
⁸ Be of sober *spirit*, be on the alert. Your adversary, the devil, prowls around like a roaring lion, seeking someone to devour.

The word sober in this context means to not be intoxicated *or* "free from illusion or intoxicating influences. Collective in spirit. Dipassionate, temperant, watchful." A big part of being sober-minded or of sober spirit is what we believe. We take in a lot of information and we see dead situations, but what we believe can either cause us to stumble or take a stand that God is sovereign and in control.

To clarify and summarize the total passage, Jesus and his disciples were not in the area when Lazarus became sick. Someone gave Jesus the message and he told the disciples that they needed to go back to Judea, he then tells them that Lazarus has died, and says "for your sake I'm glad that I wasn't there so that you may believe. Thomas says to the disciples: "Let us also go, that we may die with him." Jesus was not well liked in Judea and so Thomas resolved that wen they arrived they would be killed in Judea.

They get to Judea and Martha meets them about two miles from the tomb of Lazarus and says, "If you would have been here, my brother wouldn't have died."

Jesus says, "your brother will rise again" Martha says yes, I know he'll rise in the resurrection Jesus says, "I AM the resurrection and the life, those who believe in me, though they die, yet shall they live." Do you believe this?

Most of us know that the story ends with Jesus raising Lazarus from the dead, but one of the things that I noticed is that although Martha told Jesus that she believed, her words exhibited that her faith was not for what he could do in the present, but the promise of the Resurrection. This miracle was so much more about executing faith in the moment, and believing that Jesus who walks with us has the ability to do anything.

Reflection:
Do I really believe and trust Jesus?

Prayer:
Father, help me to realize where my faith has failed. I ask that you help my unbelief and help me to remember that you are able to do what seems impossible. Father I pray that you would highlight past circumstances where you proved yourself and power in my life and make them concrete in my memory if doubt is creeping in. I ask that you help me to be sober minded so that my thoughts are not clouded by worry, fear, or disappointment. I ask if there is any disappointment aiding in disbelief, that you would bring clarity and healing to those areas.

FURTHER REFLECTION

20

More Than a Feeling

Matthew 6:6-7
⁶ But when you pray, go into your room, close the door and pray to your Father, who is unseen. Then your Father, who sees what is done in secret, will reward you. ⁷ And when you pray, do not keep on babbling like pagans, for they think they will be heard because of their many words.

I wrote the latter part of this book at a writer's retreat that took place at a hotel with a couple of close friends. As soon as we had access to the room and decided to walk around and pray as well as check all of the closets and rooms for intruders lol. I turned on some worship music and just began to ask God to be present. I prayed for peace, protection and just that he would dwell with us.

I didn't have a tangible feeling. I didn't fall out and lay prostrate in worship. I didn't feel the urge to dance, I didn't have an emotional or physical response, I just prayed in a normal speaking voice and went on with the day.

The next day, my friend asked if I had seen how big her room was in our suite and I said, "yea I seen it when I was praying and checking the closet for tunnels that I had seen on TikTok." She said, "yea I felt the presence of the Lord and I wondered what that was about lol.

It's easy to get caught up in seeking a physical sign or emotional feeling to confirm that God hears our prayers. Sometimes we can also get caught up in performance, thinking God hears us better if we pray in a certain way.

Jesus literally tells us "not to pray with empty phrases" because your father in heaven knows what you need before you ask."

I pray this perspective encourages you. Even if you don't "feel" anything, faith is a crucial part of being a believer. Just like you have to believe that Jesus saves you, you have to believe that God hears you even if you don't have a tangible response.

Man-made doctrine will create rules of how long you should pray, and church culture may teach you that you have to sound certain way. But Jesus shows us that neither of those things matter. Nothing we do in our relationship with Christ should be about show, but it should be about service and intimacy.

Reflection:
What are practical steps that I can take to rehearse that God is with me always and that he answers prayer?

Prayer:

Father, it is only by faith that we pray and believe that you move. Please help me to remember that even if I don't feel anything, you are still there listening, loving, and moving. In a culture where we want everything to be confirmed and tangible I pray that you continue to increase my faith. I pray that you continue to give me bold faith to pray and believe that you will move according to your will. I thank you for the constant reminders that you are there when I don't experience a tangible feeling.

FURTHER REFLECTION

21

Only by Grace, Only With Faith

Ephesians 2:8-9
⁸ For by grace you have been saved through faith. And this is not your own doing; it is the gift of God, ⁹ not a result of works, so that no one may boast.

There's a culture that endorses work to gain acceptance. We can find ourselves working to gain approval of colleagues, family, even God. We go to school for others, we achieve things to say "Look, look what I've done." We do things to prove to others that we aren't who they've said we are, often to marvel at our resume's, to hold our lives up in comparison to our past and say, "it's not as bad as it used to be."

The dangerous part comes when we do this to gain our Father in heaven's acceptance. Or to prove to our brothers and sisters in Christ that we are just as good as them, *or* to prove our holiness.

I once teetered that line. Growing up in a home that was rewards and performance based I would be eager to show what I did to gain acceptance or praise. I took that into my relationship with God as I got older and thought that I had to do things to be in "right standing" with him.

I would try to set time limits to pray, try to set unattainable unauthentic goals to please the father. Most of these works that I would try to do were bred in comparison.

We see people speaking in tongues and think they're closer God, or people preaching and think they're closer to God. We see people praying for others at the altar and think they're closer to God. We see people prophesying and think that they're closer to God. The real currency of the kingdom getting you into the kingdom of God is faith and grace, those are the only two ways that we obtain anything from God.

There are many people who may not be considered righteous by a biblical standard. Works don't make you righteous. For example, in Romans 4 Paul talks about how Abraham was not justified by his works, but he believed God and that is what counted him as righteous. Without faith it is impossible to please God and comparison will kill the sincerity that we do have when it comes to being a servant of Christ. We'll find ourselves looking to our left and right to see what others are doing and try to keep up on a path that we should not have been walking on in the first place.

Reflection:
Where am I currently trying to work to gain God's

acceptance?

Prayer:

Father, I pray that you would help me to digest that works don't make me righteous. I pray that you would help me not to fall into the culture of trying to outperform others to create an image of myself that is pleasing to you. I ask that you remove all false ideas of who I think I'm supposed to be and help me to only live by the instructions in your word. Please remove all condemnation and self seeking attitudes that would hinder me from receiving and accepting your grace.

FURTHER REFLECTION

22

Let Him Have It

Matthew 16:24
²⁴ Then Jesus told his disciples, "If anyone would come after me, let him deny himself and take up his cross and follow me.

Hebrews 11:6
⁶ And without faith it is impossible to please him, for whoever would draw near to God must believe that he exists and that he rewards those who seek him.

I was reflecting on my life today and how I used to be afraid to let go of things. A part of it was fear due to a significant amount of grief that I had experienced, sometimes we can hold on to things so tightly because we don't trust God. We say that we trust, and that may be true in some areas, but when we find it difficult to let go of anything out of fear that it won't work out better it boils down to a lack of trust. A lack of faith.

We often minimize not trusting God to simply not believing

that he will do something. However, it could also be that we don't trust him just like we don't trust someone who has had a history of taking from us in the past. This is a part of the problem, seeing God as someone who takes from us, or seeing him from a carnal perspective. From the beginning, it has been God's intention to give. It's in our human nature and the result of a fallen world that we experience things being taken away.

Reflecting, I remember times where I felt the gut punch of God's voice saying to leave something behind and leave it up to me. Honestly, it wasn't until my hand was forced that I was able to relinquish control sometimes. I'm so glad that God proved himself over and over and over again. Why does God need to prove himself to us? He doesn't, but in his mercy he does. It's not even for *our* benefit sometimes that we receive what's in his will for us, but it's due to a reflection of his character and for His glory that he performs his promise.

I always see posts talking about "God is a gentleman" and I wonder where we get that from scripture because the God of Jonah, the God of Jeremiah, the God of David, and the God of Job didn't really give a choice on how they would be used. Jeremiah refusing to speak said that the word was like fire in his bones. Jonah instructed to go and minister to a nation that he had bias with was swallowed by a whale until he cried for mercy and agreed. David was minding his own business when a prophet came to his home and anointed him king without a hint that the current king was leaving the throne. Job without consent, was named God's faithful/righteous servant and was subjected to God's plan that would cause him much loss.

So will God sometimes force your hand? Scripture tells us yes, but we can make a conscious decision as well. If we just peek back, we can shift our perspective from "God is trying to take something from me," to "God is trying to accomplish his plan. If we look over our lives, we can see how our plans would've failed terribly if the Lord hadn't had intervened.

So instead of a fight with fire, a whale, or limited expectations… why not just let him do it?

Reflection:
What if anything have I been afraid to let go of? Why?

Prayer:
Father, I pray that you would help me to fully surrender to your will. I ask that you remove all hesitancy of following you and that you would help me to remember how you always have the best for me up next. I pray that you would help my heart to move without force and that my desire would be to obey you. I ask that if there is any delay associated with my obedience, that you would give me grace to move forward in your will. Forgive me for every time you had to force my hand to move forward with your plan. Help me to have faith that you have the perfect will.

FURTHER REFLECTION

23

You'll Get Back Better

Matthew 16:25
25 For whoever would save his life[a] will lose it, but whoever loses his life for my sake will find it.

Have you ever wondered "why do I keep choosing wrong?" I'm not talking about people who keep taking advantage of you or who see you as a target. I'm sharing from the perspective of actively making the wrong decisions.

I had all the support and encouragement that I needed in order to make "good" decisions growing up, but along the way I found myself making "safe" decisions. I would also make decisions that were harmful to my future. It wasn't an unanswered prayer that did it, it wasn't God not favoring me, it was me.

I kept choosing lower than what I deserved, including jobs, relationships, and different opportunities. It could be that I didn't believe that I deserved good. Instead of seeing my identity in Christ, I seen my humanity without him. I became ok with accepting less and I became ok with settling.

I settled for only receiving the bare minimum and would become frustrated when God wanted me to give up something that he *never* wanted me to settle for. Due to me never healing from this mentality, I took it into my relationship with Christ and it threatened to take over how I existed in every other space.

When a new opportunity would come I would wrestle with leaving behind the old. "Did I make the right decision?" Was always the question. There would be a hold and a feeling of grief that I had to leave someone or something behind.

The bare minimum had become a pillar, and idol that was difficult to get rid of myself. Setting people/things up as idols shows that we don't trust God to provide. Whether that be companionship, provision or even basic necessities.

When it was time to get married, God told me "I didn't send you someone with words because you are impressed by words. But I sent you someone who has the action to match." He told me that he sent me someone who hadn't been tainted by traditions of men and the rules of the church, but someone who was pure in heart and reflected 1 Corinthians 13...like Him.

Because I had conditioned myself to settle it seemed too good to be true. I almost talked myself out of what God was giving me because what was supposed to be normal had become a miracle in my eyes.

The truth is that when we accept less, it's a faith issue. When we don't want to give up something it's because we don't have faith that God has our best interest as the center of his intention. Our lack of faith in this area could be due to past things that we interpreted as a disappointment when it was most likely protection or just people failing.

I'll be honest in saying that there were points in my life where I said "God I am *tired* of always having to give up something or tired of failing in relationships. I was actually reminded of the widow in 1 Kings 17. Elijah came to her and asked for water and bread. She told him that she only had a small amount of oil and flour that she was about to prepare for her and her son and then she was preparing to die. Elijah told her to make some for herself and her son, but also told her to make a small piece for him. The promise of the Lord was that her food would not run out until the drought was lifted on their land and it didn't.

The temptation is to hold on to what you *think* the end is going to be, but the truth is that the Lord can sustain you and give you more than expected if you're willing to offer it to him.

Every time and that final time when I surrendered and prayed "I've been getting this wrong, I give it to you." I got something better. Not only that but when my desire was dismantled as an idol, when I didn't want it more than I wanted God, that's when doors started opening.

Reflection:
When did God require a sacrifice in my life without giving something in return? Is peace, joy, love, and the sanctification of obedience a sufficient return? Why or

why not?

Prayer:

Father, help me not to settle for less than what you desire for me. I pray that you would make me comfortable with the parameters and framework that you've set in place in my life. Father you have given me the guidelines to my life, and the way that I should walk. I ask that you would help me to be comfortable with what you have laid out before me. Help me to realize that your choice is the best choice. You are a great father, and I ask that you would strengthen my faith to not be attracted to what's not intended for me. Help me to trust that you do want to bless me with the desires of my heart when they align with yours. I ask that my desires be your desires, so that there is no tension in my heart between what I desire and what you have planned for me.

FURTHER REFLECTION

24

Love It or Lose It

John 12:25
²⁵ Whoever loves his life loses it, and whoever hates his life in this world will keep it for eternal life.

I can only speak for America, but I believe that we (I), (American Christians) get so caught up in our goals, in obtaining a certain lifestyle and achievements that we lose sight of eternity. I was listening to a live chat and the topic was "living life with eternity in mind." I sobered up in that moment because I had never thought to do that. We hear things like live in the moment, or even plan for the future, but a life of eternity with our father is rarely mentioned.

It could be he anxiety of not fully knowing what to expect or the temptation to believe that this world is the end to what we've been conditioned to think is the best of our lives.

Questions that could be asked to determine if we love the plan that we've hoped for more than we love God could be: Do we desire the plan more than we love spending time growing in our relationship with God? Do we desire it more than we love spending time with him? Maybe we need a perspective shift of what it means to live for Christ, to be the bridegroom waiting for the groom.

For those of us that may be dealing with the fear or intimidation of premature death, we have to remember that whenever we leave here, we are going to a much *better*, pain free, worry free, peaceful place with the God who created the heavens and the earth.

The bible does say that he will give us the desires of our hearts but then the question is: do our desires align with his?

I want to also mention that the reason that we could be struggling with the fear of not accomplishing the life that we desire, or the fear of leaving this earth is because the enemy wants to paralyze us into not doing anything at all. So, while there are people that the enemy wants to be distracted with lifetime achievements that don't necessarily give God glory, there are others that he wants to be so distracted with fear and hopelessness that they don't try to accomplish anything at all.

I was there. I got overwhelmed with the news and every time a conspiracy theory, or scary prophecy would come up I would shrink into fear and anxiety and wonder if there was any point of writing.

The point is that every day we have the opportunity contribute to bringing someone to God through Christ. Whether it be through a seed, writing, encouragement, or watering another persons seed. If you are here, it is for a reason so do not be discouraged and paralyze what God want's walking and active.

Reflection:
What am I uncomfortable giving to the Lord?

Prayer:
Father, I ask that you would rearrange my priorities. If there are areas in my life that I fear losing more than you, I ask that you would help me to change my heart posture. I pray that you reveal your love and word to me in a way that helps me to realize that there are greater things to live for than what I currently see. I pray that my heart be drawn to you and a genuine love would replace anything superficial that is occurring in my heart. Father, I pray that if the love of this life has stifled any area of productivity, that you would shine light on it and help me to accomplish what you have purposed.

FURTHER REFLECTION

25

"Jesus." Is Enough

Matthew 6:5-8
[5] "And when you pray, you must not be like the hypocrites. For they love to stand and pray in the synagogues and at the street corners, that they may be seen by others. Truly, I say to you, they have received their reward. [6] But when you pray, go into your room and shut the door and pray to your Father who is in secret. And your father who sees in secret will reward you.
[7] "And when you pray, do not heap up empty phrases as the Gentiles do, for they think that they will be heard for their many words. [8] Do not be like them, for your Father knows what you need before you ask him.

Have you ever heard someone refer to a prayer request and listen for the sound of intercession from the congregation or gathering? Then the famous words come up, "oh come on you can do better than that, pray for them the way that you would want someone to pray for you."

I was thinking of that today as I was praying for someone and all I said was "strength Lord.""Jesus." In reference to myself, I often say "Jesus," because sometimes I just don't have the "correct" words to attribute to the circumstance at that time. In one of the scariest times of my life, prayer was needed, and I simply prayed "the blood of Jesus." That's all I could say, and it worked... immediately. In times where I'm having a bad dream, I've said "Jesus" and all was well.

I think a lot of times we get caught up in man's standard and expectation of everyday things. Are there different types of prayer? Yes, but sometimes he hears the unspoken requests of our heart.The whispers of our minds, and the simplicity of our words.

I used to have a podcast called "let's just pray." In considering bringing it back, I thought about the scriptures concerning prayer. Something that comforted me when I prayed the above prayer over someone was verse 8 of the opening scripture: **"Do not be like them, for your Father knows what you need before you ask him."**

Your Father knows what you need before you ask him.

Can I be honest? I was platformed before I believe I was ready. I was opening concerts up on stages with microphones, opening services with prayer, rapid fire prayers during services, and publicly talking to God receiving praises of man for it. As a result of my immaturity, I believed that the response of the room was confirmation of me doing something right. I had mistaken it for God's approval. Man's applause was my affirmation that I was doing something good for God. People were impressed with the prayers, but it was the anointing of God, and sometimes his grace. I started looking into this scripture and being comforted that I don't even have to have all of the eloquent speech and all of the right words. I just have to talk because he already knows before I ask.Are there principles and examples of prayers, and even strategies? Yes. Absolutely. But the heart behind why you're praying what you're praying is what matters most.

Reflection:
Where have I over complicated prayer out of religious teaching or lack of faith that God won't hear/answer my simple words?

Prayer:
Father, I ask that you remove all practices that I have adopted that are not from you. I pray that you help me to remember the foundation of your word, the intentions of your teachings on prayer, and your desire just to commune with us as your children. Father, I ask that you increase my faith in the simple things. Help me to remember that you hear me so that when I pray I believe that you hear and will respond.

FURTHER REFLECTION

26

Eternal LIFE

1 Peter 5:10
[10] And after you have suffered a little while, the God of all grace, who has called you to his eternal glory in Christ, will himself restore, confirm, strengthen, and establish you.

This is a book about different perspectives, right? I have experienced a lot of loss in my life. My mother passed away when I was 3 months old, my paternal grandmother passed away when I was 14 years old, my father passed away when I was 21, my maternal grandfather passed away when I was 22, and my maternal grandmother passed away when I was 25.

Up until recently I was somewhat crippled with the fear of death, or just fear in general. I had this prayer that I would pray every single night from as early as I could remember. I would cover everyone close to me in prayer. I would pray prayers of protection and good health. I would ask God specific prayers about my grandparents being able to live to see certain things.

I would cover my father and our home, even riding my bike, I would pray. Although the prayers were rooted in fear, I would pray that I wouldn't see dogs, bees or anything that could harm me. My prayer life, before I even openly accepted Christ out loud in front of others, had been established as early as age 8 or 9 years old out of fear.

It's 2024, and it wasn't until very recently that God began to change my perspective on death, and it could be because I stopped relying on man for comfort. I wanted a new foundation outside of running scared to others all the time. By doing that, I've had more peace than chaos in my mind. I am super grateful for that, and its evidence that I've come a long way over the years.

I would get so frustrated with constantly reading things like "life is short," "Live now," "Anything can happen any second." It wasn't until recently that I understood that it wasn't me that was frustrated, but it was my spirit.

The truth is, life isn't short, it's eternal. The truth is that whatever we experience on earth cannot compare to what we will experience in eternity (Romans 8:18). We also must remember that we are not in control of our lives and that everything is going to be ok. Most of all we must remember that everything being ok might mean that it will be ok *eventually*. As tough as that is, taking inventory of your hardships and remembering that you are on the other side of some or all of them is a good way to relax and fall into the Father. Really digesting the word-the bread of life into your heart to remember who he is to us is essential for peace of mind. Jesus tells us not to worry about tomorrow, let's really soak in what he's saying and cast our cares to him.

Reflection:
Have I reconciled that God's presence is the *best* place to be, outside of what we believe that we can feel tangibly?

Prayer:
Father, help me to reconcile that being with you here and later is the best place I can be. I pray that you would remove all fear and misunderstanding that would seek to derail me from the present. I ask that you would help me to relinquish control over my life and restore my confidence in you. I pray that you would refresh my understanding of your word that would comfort me and direct my path. I pray that you would help me to focus on you, so that I won't sink while attempting.

FURTHER REFLECTION

27

Your Reason Matters

Acts 8:18-20
[18] Now when Simon saw that the Spirit was given through the laying on of the apostles' hands, he offered them money, [19] saying, "Give me this power also, so that anyone on whom I lay my hands may receive the Holy Spirit." [20] But Peter said to him, "May your silver perish with you, because you thought you could obtain the gift of God with money!

There was a point in my life where I was in a culture that contributed to me wanting to speak in tongues just to shut people up. I wanted to prove I had the holy spirit. I was very sharp with the word, and I received visions from God to execute in the group that I was leader of. So much so that the glory of God would fall, heal, and deliver others. Rooms would be stuck forced to wait on instructions from Holy Spirit on how to move forward, that's of no credit to myself.

I remember someone asking me how I would come up with

choreography, I said "God", and they rolled their eyes as if I was trying to be "deep." It was the truth though, and I love those creative spaces with God. I had a relationship with him, a heart to do what he wanted and I believe that is why I was trusted with those moments. At the same time there started to be conversations about how "I didn't have Holy Spirit." I became frustrated because I knew I had a close relationship with God, we spoke often.

In the beginning, I desired speaking in tongues because I wanted another level of intimacy, once I started talking to other believers the desire became perverted. It became about showing others that I was just as saved as them because I was tired of hearing about it. It wasn't because I desired deeper intimacy anymore. Don't allow others to invalidate your relationship with God in an attempt for them to feel better about how they believe you should look for ministry.

The moment my heart & motive changed, and I got out of that culture I spoke in tongues.

I was in a small room with a smaller ministry. Their motives were pure. It wasn't about proof. It was about ushering someone deeper into their relationship with Christ. It was about a God led unction to ask a question about a desire of my heart that had been suppressed due to religion.

I remember someone asking "have you received your heavenly language? I said "no," ready to feel defeated again. Someone else asked "why?" I said something to the effect of "I don't believe that it'll happen."

Someone said, "Just praise God." Not "Say Jesus over and over and over again." My friend placed her hand on my back, and I began to speak what sounded like a stutter. Immediately, when doubt began to creep in, someone prayed against doubt.

Comparison started coming during services and I immediately wanted to sound different, but as soon as I desired it for the wrong reasons the same problems began to rise up. The moment I had a heart change, it changed.

Motive matters, your reasons for wanting things, even spiritual things matter. We shouldn't want experiences and gifts of God for power but for *his* glory and for relationship with him.

Reflection:
Are there any areas in my walk with Christ where I am tempted to perform before men instead of being sincere with the Father?

Prayer:
Father, I pray that my desire to commune with you is greater than my desire to prove myself to others. I ask that you purify my heart of any rubric that I have tried to live up to that is not yours. I ask that you would help me to know that the condition of my relationship with you is priority. Father, help my desires to be close to you to be pure. Cleanse my heart from any temptation to show "who I am" in you.

FURTHER REFLECTION

28

Don't Worry & Rush

Philippians 1:6 ESV
And I am sure of this, that he who began a good work in you will bring it to completion at the day of Jesus Christ.

Psalm 46:9-10
remember the former things of old;
for I am God, and there is no other;
I am God, and there is none like me,
declaring the end from the beginning
and from ancient times things not yet done,
saying, 'My counsel shall stand,
and I will accomplish all my purpose,'

Has there been a situation where you were the expert on the topic, and you knew the timing of what needed to be done, but it didn't match up with the expectations of who was asking?

Have you ever been in a situation where you were asked to do something and you had the ability to do it, but the requester tried to control when it was going to be accomplished? I'm not talking about instances where you were negligent, or you didn't have the capacity or the skill to do it.

For Example, you as a creator of what the person was asking, gave a yes, or an answer without a deadline. Some would call that irresponsible but there are concrete and flexible deadlines.

Sometimes the things that we ask God for are simply a waiting game. I often pray for long life, to be able to see my kids grow, for them to remain in our care, for them not to have the same story as me, do you know what God said to me?

"This type of promise, you have no choice except to wait it out. If you spend all of this time worrying *if* it's going to happen, you're going to look up *in* the promise, add up the time that was wasted worrying, and see what all you could've done with it that is actually productive."

Imagine having the audacity to rush the *author* and finisher of our faith.

Reflection:
What situation do I have right now that makes me anxious about whether or not God is going to do it?

Prayer:
Father you are the author and the finisher or my faith. I recognize that I will never have all of the answer and timings of my life. I pray that you would increase my faith in this area and help me to trust in you when it feels

like things are not happening at the pace that I would like them. I pray that for the promises that require time, you would drop reminders of you being there along the way. I believe that because you are the creator of all things, and you are all knowing, that you have the best planned for me as your child. Help me to rest in your promises.

FURTHER REFLECTION

29

God Precedes Us

Joshua 2:11
And as soon as we heard it, our hearts melted, and there was no spirit left in any man because of you, for the Lord your God, he is God in the heavens above and on the earth beneath.

I love the story of Joshua. I found in reading it that I minimized it to the Israelite's entering the promised land, which *is* a big deal. However, like other times in reading scripture I glanced over a key detail of the story of Rahab. It's often told that Joshua sends to spies into Jericho, Rahab hides them, they make a promise that her family will be safe, she takes the scarlet chord hangs it outside her window, they march around seven times, they shout, the wall falls down, Rahab is found safe, they enter the land, amen.

That's how I've heard it and remembered it. More recently I've seen the memes on social media about Rahab's name changing from "prostitute" to "great grandmother of Jesus." This is great, but there is a key factor that I and many others are missing out on. The stories of him destroying their enemies in the past were a staple in the mind of those in that territory. Not only were the stories of him destroying their enemies known, but his faithfulness and power to deliver them as well as his love for them. The scripture says that after Rahab hid the spies, and the men of her city came after them, she went up to them and told them:

Joshua 2: 9-11
And she said unto the men, I know that the Lord hath given you the land, and that your terror is fallen upon us, and that all the inhabitants of the land faint because of you.
10 For we have heard how the Lord dried up the water of the Red sea for you, when ye came out of Egypt; and what ye did unto the two kings of the Amorites, that were on the other side Jordan, Sihon and Og, whom ye utterly destroyed.
11 And as soon as we had heard these things, our hearts did melt, neither did there remain any more courage in any man, because of you: for the Lord your God, he is God in heaven above, and in earth beneath.

Gods character and power preceded the people of Israel entering into Jericho. Their enemies, although against them, knew the power of their God and it caused their enemies to not have courage. Our God is so powerful that when we belong to him those against us or those in possession of what he has given us can see how he has moved for us. Frequently we hear messages of how we have an enemy and we can become so enemy focused that we forget that we serve a more powerful God. A part of maturing as a believer is focus. Not Focusing on what's in front of us, but who our God is. Once we shift our perspective to making God the primary focus everything becomes smaller.

The message that the spies were left with to take back to Joshua was:

Joshua 2:24
24 And they said to Joshua, "Truly the Lord has given all the land into our hands. And also, all the inhabitants of the land melt away because of us.

In other words, not only does his promise for this land still stand, those that are in what belongs to us fear our God because he's made his name known on our behalf. I believe that's an awesome nugget of faith that they had the opportunity to take with them before they took over the city.

Reflection:
Where has my history with God made a declaration? How does knowing that God has a reputation with my adversity affect my perspective towards my challenges?

Prayer:
Father, thank you for going before me. Thank you for your reputation and history of your love that proves your faithfulness. I pray that you use my memory as a weapon against any fear or worry. I thank you that your unfailing

love for me, and your inability to not fail have served as a pillar in my history with you. Thank you for your mercy, your grace, and your moves making such an impact in my life. I pray for an increase of faith to stand in any challenges before I see my promise.

FURTHER REFLECTION

30

Study, Well.

In order to not contribute to a chaotic home (see "chaotic home" entry), as I'm preparing to publish this book I wanted to share what sparked the idea. I was scrolling on social media and I would see statuses that took scripture out of context and out of frustration I would want to post a response. I found that to be irresponsible so instead of immediately responding I would go study what I thought was the correct response. Instead of writing that status or comment, I leaned into the fact that every time I wanted to respond I would feel the push to just "put it in a book."

Sometimes our initial thoughts about the scripture can be a temptation to serve as is. It can be thrilling to serve it as an appetizer or fast food, but the word of God is not so surface level that it can be served like that. I think that we would be better if we actually digested what we consumed instead of immediately regurgitating it. We would be a healthier body. How do we expect to put on weight if we are constantly throwing up what takes time to consume. It takes study and time, and if our initial thoughts aren't the thoughts of God they can actually be poison to others. We have to know that reading scripture with only the heart to prove others wrong, debate, and make ourselves feel good is not the goal of studying scripture. Thinking that the scripture is a weapon to use against others in times of disagreement goes against us needing to be one body.

It is imperative to develop a life of study just for intimacy with God. To sum up the heart of this book would be to say that we have a responsibility as believers to not read the bible from our cultural mindset, but to find out the heart behind what God is saying in scripture. We should take a look at scripture from point in history and culture that was present at that time listening to Holy Spirit for correct application.

So as we finish up this journey of considering other perspectives, re-learning, and taking another look. I would like to leave you with some tools that I use to study the bible to ensure or try to make sure that I am not reading out of an incorrect lens.

1. Biblehub.com
2. Blueletterbible.com
3. Bible Project.com
4. Strongs Concordance
5. Vines Dictionary

Reflection:
What's one tool that I can implement to study scripture?
Where have I had challenges in understanding the Bible?

Prayer:

Father, if there is any intention other than knowing you better when it comes to me studying your Word, I ask that you remove them and renew my heart. I ask that your scripture comes a live to me as I read and that you share your heart with me. I pray that you correct all false teachings and help me to have an open mind to what you want to teach me. I ask that you shift my priorities in studying your word, that you change my heart to desire intimacy and not debate. I pray that you help me to have a desire for you, above everything else.

FURTHER REFLECTION

Acknowledgement

I wrote my first book when I was single, no kids, and only had distractions that I created myself. I wrote my second book (unpublished) very quickly and because it was short it was a breath of fresh air. My third book I wrote with a newborn baby attached to me, trying to figure out the self-publishing process, and all of the things that come with it. This book, I wrote during pockets of time in the night where there was quiet. I wrote it with many interruptions, pauses, and the frustration of just wanting to get it done. However, it was in one of those moments of frustration during a pause that I heard the whisper of Holy Spirit say: "if this isn't taken care of, then the book doesn't matter."

So I would like to acknowledge my family. Thank you for your patience, your grace, and the lessons a long the way. To my husband, who would tell me to "just go and lock the door," thank you for your covering, love and grace. To my bouncing toddlers who would pop into the room as soon as I would open my laptop to work, thank you for the reminder of priority.

While this book was written in what seems like a whirlwind, I remember words from Apostle Stephanie Page that were spoken years before this book was even thought of. She told me that in the busyness of life I would look up, look back and wonder how I got it done, and these are my exact sentiments for this book that was written in a little under 6 months. Thank you for your push to always rely on God's strength and not my own.

About the Author

Brittney Davis was born and raised in Saginaw, MI. She is a spoken word artist and owner of Ready Writer Books. Brittney began writing through journaling as early as six years old as a means to cope with trauma and later found a love for expressing herself through creative words. Her passions include using creativity to reach the unreachable and showing the love of Christ to those who need it the most. Through her writing she strives to let others know that they are not alone with a goal of creating a safe space for those who deal with the pains of grief, heartache and life happenings. Brittney Charisse prides herself on being versatile and flexible with content in order to touch hearts and lead them to a greater resolve, Jesus. She has graced the stage in college classrooms, conferences, high schools, churches and local venues across the nation with one thing in mind: "What you say on stage is only half of your impact, but it's also about what you say when you step off of the stage."

Also by Brittney Davis

Available at www.readywriterbooks.com and Amazon

Fathered (2020)
Fathered is a metaphorical journey of spirituality. Brittney Davis Parallels the endearing relationship she shared with her now departed father with the relationship she is continually experiencing with God, the Father. She reveals to readers how having a close-knit, loving, supportive, corrective, and protective experience with her natural father helped her understand how God shows himself as Father to us in ways we sometimes don't recognize. God is not a detached ruler in the heavens who looks down in juedgement-he is present and his heart beats for his children.

Ready Writer (2023)
Ready Writer is the author's journey through her life as a poet and spoken word artist. This work features the ups and downs of life in poetry form and the evolution of the author as a writer. Brittney Charisse offers what may be missed at the mic in her "Before the Microphone" sections and also gives a glimpse into the mind behind the artist. Travel with her through different topics, hardships, and lessons as she unfolds them through the art of writing.